Christmas in Nature's Playground

A Festive Story, Songs, Crafts and Recipes

Written and Illustrated by Emily Ifsits

For my Children – for the magic that you bring to life at Christmas time and always.

ISBN: 978-3-9505009-4-3

As a teacher and mum of two, I have had the privilege of spending many Christmases with excited young children. Through Christmas stories, crafts, songs, and baking I have created many lovely festive memories.

I hope that sharing this book with your children or pupils brings you joy and inspires you to create special memories too.

Wishing you a very Merry Christmas!

Emily Ifsits

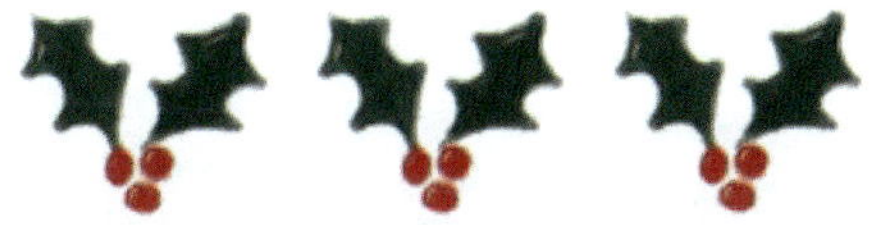

Contents

Story

The Deer Who Saved Christmas – p.6-15

Recipes

Gingerbread Smores – p.16-18

Honey Punch – p.19

Sleigh Riding Songs

Pulling Santa's Sleigh – p.20

Flying High Above the Roofs – p.21

Salt Dough Crafts

Recipe – p.22

Reindeer – p.23-24

Robins – p.25-26

Festive Bird Feeders – p.27-30

The Deer Who Saved Christmas

On a night when all of the homes were alight

With colourful trees glistening bright.

I heard the jingle of bells passing by,

A sleigh and eight reindeer were high in the sky!

The driver in red, looked friendly and round,

He saw me below and came down to the ground.

“I’m Santa and looking for help”, he said,

“My reindeer must rest, do you have a nice bed?”

His reindeer was looking really quite sleepy,

Snuffling and coughing, a little bit weepy.

"I do," I replied, "I'll take him to mother,

He'll be safe and snug with my small baby brother."

"Thank you, kind deer, and now we must fly,

Come on, now reindeer, up to the sky!"

They lurched and they heaved then collapsed on the ground,

"With one reindeer missing, we're stuck!" Santa frowned.

"Oh no! Oh bother! This really can't be,

All of the children are counting on me!"

"Don't be sad, Santa, we'll soon find a way....

...teach me to fly and *I'll* pull your sleigh!"

First came a swirl of sparkling dust,

Then on with the reins, then came a strong thrust.

Forwards I flew, then up and around,

Around and around till I bumped on the ground!

The sun was rising, with time running out,

I kept on trying, "I'll do it!" I shout.

"Close your eyes," said one reindeer, "and I'll lead you up high,

Hold onto my tail, 'til we reach the night sky".

With a wobble and whoosh, we shot over the trees,

I started to tremble and shake in my knees.

The sleigh jerked right, and Santa yelled, "Steady!

Come on woodland deer, you can do this, you're ready".

"Just look to the stars and not to the ground,

Take a deep breath, and hear the sweet sound

Of the wind past your ears inside of this cloud,

The rustling of gifts and the bells jingling proud."

"Let's work together, for the girls and the boys,

For the magic of stockings with shiny new toys."

I steadied my breath, and did as he said,
Just listened and fear drifted out of my head,
And out of my knees and shivering hooves,
As I felt the slow beat, my legs knew the moves.

My heart soon soared with joy and with pride,
"I'm flying, I'm flying, I'm flying!" I cried.
With a whistle and whoop, Santa called, "Yay!
Your kindness and courage have saved Christmas Day!"
Before flying home, my friends came to stay
For breakfast with me, the woodland deer way.

We made gingerbread smores

and hot honey punch.

The poorly reindeer, now better, took extra for lunch.

Then off flew my friends back into the sky,

“Thank you! Merry Christmas! Cheerio and Goodbye!”

But each Christmas Eve, they come by to munch

Our sweet sticky smores with the gingerbread crunch.

Gingerbread Smores

Ingredients

125g salted butter

4 tbsp golden syrup

175g light brown sugar

1 tsp bicarbonate of soda

2 tsp ground ginger

1 tsp ground cinnamon

350g plain flour

1 egg

1 packet of marshmallows

Method

1. Sift the flour, bicarbonate of soda, ginger, and cinnamon into a bowl.

2. Mix the golden syrup and egg together and add them to the dry ingredients.

3. Knead the dough until smooth, then form a ball.

4. Wrap it in cling film and pop it in the fridge for 15 minutes.

5. Roll the dough out until 0.5cm thick on a floured surface.

6. Cut out your biscuits into festive shapes.

7. Bake them at 180C/160C Fan/Gas until they are a light golden brown (12-15 minutes).

8. Toast your marshmallows on your campfire, squish them between your biscuits and enjoy them!

Honey Punch

Ingredients

1 litre of apple juice

1 cinnamon stick

3 Cloves

Honey

Method

1. Heat the apple juice, cinnamon sticks and cloves together in a pan over your campfire.
2. Add honey and stir until it is sweet enough for you.

Pulling Santa's Sleigh

(to the tune of Jingle Bells)

Flying through the sky,
Pulling Santa on his sleigh,
The cold wind rushing by,
Laughing all the way!

The jingle bells we ring,
Loud and proud we play,
Oh, what fun it is to pull
Santa on his sleigh!

Hey jingle bells, jingle bells,
Jingle all the way,
Oh, what fun it is to pull
Santa on his sleigh! (x2)

Flying High Above the Roofs

(To the tune of Twinkle, Twinkle, Little Star)

Leaping high into to the air,
Gifts all wrapped for us to share.

Twinkling stars light our way,
Guide us till the light of day.

Leaping high into to the air,
Gifts all wrapped for us to share.

Flying, flying over roofs,
Galloping on magic hooves.

Twinkling stars light our way,
Guide us till the light of day.

Flying, flying over roofs,
Galloping on magic hooves.

Jingle Sticks

These jingle sticks make wonderful instruments and are the perfect accompaniment when singing sleigh riding songs!

1. Hunt for sticks of whatever size you fancy. Larger ones are also great for banging on the ground instead of shaking.

2. Wrap whatever ribbon, thick string or material that you have around the stick. Weave little bells (and any other festive decorations) as you go.

Salt Dough Recipe

Ingredients

250g Flour

125g Salt

125ml Water

1. Add all the ingredients into a bowl.
2. Squeeze, gather and knead the mixture with your hands until you can form nice smooth balls of dough. (Add more water or flour as needed.)

Salt Dough Reindeer

1. Collect some twigs, stones, and greenery that you would like to include on your reindeer.

2. Mould your salt dough into a sitting reindeer shape.

3. Add your natural materials to create your reindeer's legs, antlers, and eyes.

4. Let your reindeer air dry and then paint them.

Salt Dough Robins

1. Collect twigs for your robin's nest.

2. Create a base for your robin to sit on by squashing a ball of salt dough flat.

3. Roll a small ball of dough for the head and pinch a little beak shape. Roll a larger ball of dough for the body and pinch a tail shape. Then stick the head to the body, smoothing the two together with your fingers.

4. Push the twigs into the base to make the nest.

5. Allow to air dry and then paint your robin.

Festive Bird Feeders

Ingredients

Mixed seeds

Raisins

Unsalted nuts

Cooked rice

Hard cheese

Lard

Method

1. Mix all of the dry ingredients in a bowl and then add enough lard to bind it all together.

Now prepare festive containers to pack it in. Here are a couple of ideas...

An old mug with festive foliage and a Christmas bauble or other decoration that is going spare or

a plastic cup or yogurt pot decorated with foliage, ribbons and baubles using a hot glue gun.

2. Add the bird food into your containers, packing it in nice and tightly.

3. Finally, add a little stick so that the birds can comfortably perch as they enjoy their meal. It will also help you to watch them as they feed.

Emily Ifsits

Emily Ifsits is a graduate of the University of York with a degree in Educational Studies and has a Post Graduate Certificate of Education from the University of Exeter. She has a Level 3 BTEC Advanced Award Forest School Leaders qualification from Bridgewater College.

She was an early years teacher for 8 years, in England. She was the head of the reception year group, Forest School leader and the reception music teacher in Clifton College Pre-Preparatory School, Bristol.

Emily now lives in Austria where she is beginning a new chapter in her career as a Montessori teacher. Her greatest passion is escaping into the great outdoors on adventures with her husband and two young children.

And she loves Christmas.

Also, by Emily Ifsits:

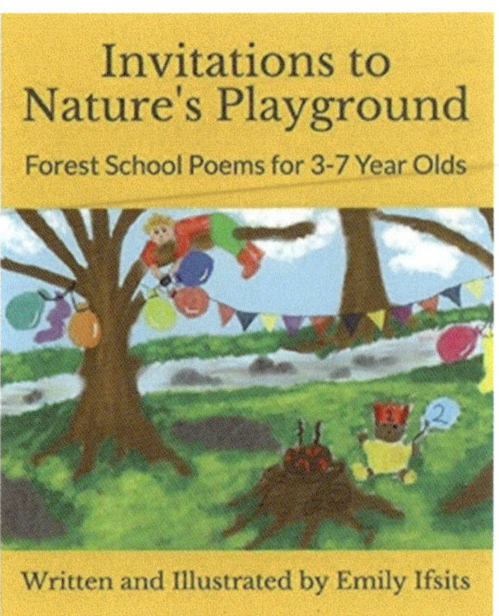

Available worldwide on Amazon.

You can stay up-to-date with Emily Ifsits' new publications by subscribing to the monthly newsletter on her author webpage: **www.emilyifsits.com**.

You can also follow her on her Welly Days Facebook page where she shares ideas for outdoor play.

Printed in Great Britain
by Amazon

71166183R00020